101 Gourmet cake bites

FOR all OCCASIONS

WENDY PAUL

FRONT TABLE BOOKS
SPRINGVILLE, UTAH

ISBN: 978-1-4621-4088-6

Published by Front Table Books, an imprint of Cedar Fort, Inc., 2373 W. 700 S., Springville, UT 84663
Distributed by Cedar Fort, Inc., www.cedarfort.com

THE LIBRARY OF CONGRESS HAS CATALOGED THE HARDBACK EDITION AS FOLLOWS:
Paul, Wendy, author.
101 gourmet cake bites / Wendy Paul.
p. cm.
Summary: Recipes for cake bites -- little pieces of cake baked using a mix, rolled into balls, and covered with icing.
ISBN 978-1-59955-895-0
1. Cake. 2. Cooking, American. I. Title.

TX771.P376 2011
641.5973--dc22

2011005381

Cover and page design by Angela D. Olsen
Cover design © 2011 by Lyle Mortimer
Edited by Heidi Doxey

Printed in the United States of America

10 9 8 7 6 5 4 3 2

Printed on acid-free paper

Dedication

TO MY CHILDREN...

Thank you for your hugs and kisses each and every day. I can't imagine a better job than being your mom. You are the best taste testers in the world.

I LOVE YOU!

Contents

Holiday Treats

Theme Decorating

The Icing Inside the Little Bites

Fall in Love at First Bite

LITTLE DID I KNOW that a sweet treat could have me hooked at first bite. These little cake bites are a mouthful of happiness and pleasure and they tickle your taste buds delightfully.

CAKE BITES ARE PLAYFUL, yet sophisticated. They are perfect for weddings, birthday parties, graduations, or any special occasion. You can even make them "just because."

REMEMBER, THERE IS ALWAYS a reason to bake!

BY USING A CAKE MIX, and adding a few extra ingredients to make it gourmet, these little cake bites will not only look great but taste great too! From Piña Colada to Root Beer Float, Pumpkin Cheesecake to Dark Chocolate Truffle, these cake bites are amazing little masterpieces.

HAPPY BAKING!

—Wendy L. Paul

Getting Started

THINGS YOU WILL NEED

- One cake, baked, cooled, and crumbled.
- Large mixing bowl
- Big spoon
- Small cookie scoop
- 1lb. melting chocolate per batch of cake bites plus vegetable oil
- 2 forks or spoons for dipping cake bites into melting chocolate
- Wax paper for cooling
- Sucker sticks for cake pops
- Foam for sticking cake pops in to set
- Sprinkles or toppings for cake bites
- Other decorating supplies, pens, toothpicks, and so on (per recipe directions).

Tips *for* Success

CAKE BALLS, CAKE BITES, CAKE POPS, EVEN CUPCAKE POPS. What's the difference? Well, it's simple, really. It's all a matter of design.

CAKE BALLS are just that. Little pieces of cake rolled into a ball. Then covered in chocolate and placed on a large platter, waiting to be devoured. Size varies from small to medium to large.

CAKE BITES, for all intents and purposes, are just a cake ball that is bite size—ready to snatch up in one bite. Cake bites are usually the size of a quarter, rounded.

CAKE POPS? Well, that's where it gets a little trickier. But still easy as pie, or should I say cake? Shape the cake into a small bite-size cake bite, then stick a candy stick into the bottom. Chill to set the cake pop.

CUPCAKE POPS—I had to include these since I am known as Mrs. Cupcake. . . . By using a small cupcake mold, you can shape your cake pop into a cupcake. I found my molds online, but they are also available at most cake decorating supply stores. And they're absolutely adorable!

YOU WILL NEED foam to stick the cake pop into once it has been decorated.

FORMING & SHAPING THE CAKE BITES.

Size really does matter here. This is done much like shaping a meatball—only the result is much sweeter. It is best if your hands are clean, so be sure to wash and dry them several times during the rolling process. If you are having a hard time keeping the balls uniform in size, don't be afraid to use a small cookie scoop to get the right amount of cake into your hand. The perfect size is a quarter, rounded in the palm of your hand.

Once the cake bite is formed, place it on a cookie sheet in rows, and refrigerate for 1–2 hours, or freeze for 20 minutes to harden the cake bite. Chilling the bites makes it easier and faster to dip them in the chocolate.

FREEZING CAKE BITES

These little pieces of heaven freeze just as well as a piece of cake. For several months at least (if you can keep them that long!) Place your rolled cake bites on a baking sheet and freeze in a single layer, not touching. Freeze until set (usually 1 hour). Then remove your frozen cake bites and place them in a freezer bag. Be sure to label and date. When you are ready to eat your cake bites, pull out what you need, melt your chocolate, and away you go!

THE MELTING CHOCOLATE

Over the course of baking these fantastic cake bites, I have learned that it is best if you add 1–2 tablespoons of vegetable oil to your 1 lb. of melting chocolate or candy coating. It gives a smoother consistency, and a thinner shell of chocolate coating—which my taste testers and I preferred. Also, it's important when dipping your cake bites to keep the melting chocolate hot. If it starts to cool, the chocolate will thicken, making the dipping harder and more lumpy. No one wants a lumpy cake bite!

COATING THE CAKE BITES WITH CHOCOLATE.

Follow the directions on the package of melting chocolate, also known as candy chocolate. Be sure to melt only a small amount at a time, that way the chocolate will stay easier to work with. You can always melt more chocolate if needed. Then using either 2 spoons, or forks (I prefer using forks), take the cake bite, and dip it into the melting chocolate, covering the entire surface. Do not roll the cake bite around, as this can leave crumbs in the melting chocolate. Remove the cake bite carefully and tap the fork on the edge of the bowl gently to release any excess chocolate from the cake bite.

Then transfer the cake bite to wax paper to set. To avoid fingerprints on your cake bite chocolate, wear candy-making gloves. Top with any candies or garnish before the chocolate is set.

At first this will feel a bit awkward, but as you finish the process, you will develop your own groove, and you will be a champ at dipping cake bites!

HOW MANY CAKE BITES WILL I GET?

This really depends on the size you shape your cake bites. Usually a typical recipe can make 36–40 cake bites when shaped in the size of a rounded quarter. If you make medium-sized cake bites the same recipe will yield about 32 servings. And if you make large cake bites (golf-ball sized) it will yield about 26–28.

If you don't want that many cake bites, you can quarter the recipe. Just simply use ¼ of your baked cake, and ¼ the frosting and add-ins you have chosen. You can freeze the remaining cake for another time. Seal the remaining cake in an airtight bag and label.

When you bake a lighter cake, such as white, yellow, pink, or green, you will notice golden brown flecks around all the sides of the cake. Be sure to carefully slice away any golden brown edges and flecks. This will make your cake a brighter, truer color. Note: when you slice away some of the cake, be sure to adjust the frosting amount. Decrease by ¼–⅓ cup for the recipe. Then add more if needed.

Fruity and Fabulous

Key Lime Pie

Key Lime Pie

I know that this may be difficult for you to imagine, so you are going to have to bake these little cake bites for yourself. Either that or move into a home for sale in my neighborhood so I can bring you some regularly.

1 box yellow cake mix

½ Tbsp. grated lime zest

⅓ cup key lime juice

¾ cup half-and-half

2 eggs

MIX TOGETHER cake mix, lime zest, key lime juice, half-and-half, and eggs. Batter will be thick. Pour into a greased 9x13 baking pan. Bake at 350 degrees for 28–32 minutes or until cake springs back when lightly touched. Remove from oven and cool completely. Crumble cake into small, even pieces, placing crumbs in a large bowl.

ADD

¼ cup Lime Buttercream Frosting (130)

½ cup sweetened condensed milk

2 Tbsp. grated lime zest

MAKES 26–40

WITH THE BACK of a spoon, mix together cake crumbles with other ingredients until a thick dough consistency forms. Shape into evenly sized cake bites (xi) and cool 1–2 hours in the refrigerator, or 20 minutes in the freezer. Dip into white melting chocolate (xii). Top with crushed graham crackers if desired.

Lemon Poppy Seed

A cake bite that tastes like a great muffin you'd get from your favorite deli. I think you could have these cake bites for breakfast—I won't tell anyone.

1 box lemon cake mix

1 tsp. lemon extract

1 Tbsp. poppy seeds

3 eggs

¾ cup milk

MIX TOGETHER cake mix, lemon extract, poppy seeds, eggs, and milk. Batter will be thick. Pour into a greased 9x13 baking pan. Bake at 350 degrees for 28–32 minutes or until cake springs back when lightly touched. Remove from oven and cool completely. Crumble cake into small, even pieces, placing crumbs in a large bowl.

ADD

1 cup Lemon Buttercream Frosting (137)

2 Tbsp. grated lemon zest

MAKES 26–40

WITH THE BACK of a spoon, mix together cake crumbles with other ingredients until a thick dough consistency forms. Shape into evenly sized cake bites (xi) and cool 1–2 hours in the refrigerator or 20 minutes in the freezer. Dip into melting chocolate (xii). Serve.

Piña Colada

I'm sitting in a lounge chair, listening to the ocean surf crash around me . . . as I eat these cake bites . . . the warm sun heating touching my skin . . . . Oh, wait. It's snowing. Reality check! Anytime you want to take a little vacation—pop a Piña Colada cake bite in your mouth.

1 box white cake mix

3 eggs

½ cup lite coconut milk

½ cup pineapple juice

1 tsp. coconut extract

2 tablespoons flour

MIX TOGETHER cake mix, eggs, coconut milk, pineapple juice, coconut extract, and flour. Batter will be thick. Pour into a greased 9x13 baking pan. Bake at 350 degrees for 28–32 minutes or until cake springs back when lightly touched. Remove from oven and cool completely. Crumble cake into small, even pieces, placing crumbs in a large bowl.

ADD

1 cup Coconut Buttercream Frosting (133)

2 Tbsp. dried pineapple chunks, finely diced

shredded coconut

MAKES 26–40

WITH THE BACK of a spoon, mix together cake crumbles with other ingredients until a thick dough consistency forms. Shape into evenly sized cake bites (xi) and cool 1–2 hours in the refrigerator, or 20 minutes in the freezer. Dip into melting chocolate (xii) and sprinkle with shredded coconut (optional). While eating, dream of your own tropical paradise.

Coconut Cream Pie

ALSO PICTURED (L TO R): New York Cheesecak and Rosemary Lavende

Coconut Cream Pie

When I was younger, I couldn't stand the taste or texture of coconut. Now that I am older and wiser, I love it in almost anything. Chicken dishes, desserts, cakes, pies, and especially cake bites. What was I thinking?

1 box white cake mix

1 tsp. coconut extract

¾ cup lite coconut milk

3 eggs

2 Tbsp. flour

MIX TOGETHER cake mix, coconut extract, coconut milk, eggs, and flour. Batter will be thick. Pour into a greased 9x13 baking pan. Bake at 350 degrees for 28–32 minutes or until cake springs back when lightly touched. Remove from oven and cool completely. Crumble cake into small, even pieces, placing crumbs in a large bowl.

ADD

8 oz. cream cheese, softened

¼ cup Coconut Buttercream Frosting (133)

Shredded coconut for garnish

MAKES 26–40

WITH THE BACK of a spoon, mix together cake crumbles with other ingredients until a thick dough consistency forms. Shape into evenly sized cake bites (xi) and cool 1–2 hours in the refrigerator, or 20 minutes in the freezer. Dip into white melting chocolate (xii). Top with toasted or sweetened shredded coconut.

Lemon Cream Pie

What good is a cookbook in your kitchen without a great lemon treat inside? Sweet, tart, fun, and a little sassy. . . . I like sassy.

1 box lemon cake mix

2 Tbsp. grated lemon zest

3 eggs

1 tsp. lemon extract

¾ cup half-and-half

MIX TOGETHER cake mix, lemon zest, eggs, lemon extract, and half-and-half. Batter will be thick. Pour into a greased 9x13 baking pan. Bake at 350 degrees for 28–32 minutes or until cake springs back when lightly touched. Remove from oven and cool completely. Crumble cake into small, even pieces, placing crumbs in a large bowl.

ADD

⅓ cup crushed hard lemon candy

8 oz. cream cheese, softened

¼ cup Lemon Buttercream Frosting (137)

2 Tbsp. grated lemon zest

MAKES 26–40

WITH THE BACK of a spoon, mix together cake crumbles with other ingredients until a thick dough consistency forms. Shape into evenly sized cake bites (xi) and cool 1–2 hours in the refrigerator or 20 minutes in the freezer. Dip into white melting chocolate (xii).

Raspberry Lemonade

Hot. Summer. Swimming. Raspberry Lemonade. They all go hand in hand.

1 box lemon cake mix

3 eggs

¾ cup half-and-half

1 tsp. lemon extract

MIX TOGETHER cake mix, eggs, half-and-half, and lemon extract. Batter will be thick. Pour into a greased 9x13 baking pan. Bake at 350 degrees for 28–32 minutes or until cake springs back when lightly touched. Remove from oven and cool completely. Crumble cake into small, even pieces, placing crumbs in a large bowl.

ADD

1 cup Vanilla Buttercream Frosting (125)

2 Tbsp. grated lemon zest

2 tsp. raspberry flavoring

WITH THE BACK of a spoon, mix together cake crumbles with other ingredients until a thick dough consistency forms. Shape into evenly sized cake bites (xi) and cool 1–2 hours in the refrigerator, or 20 minutes in the freezer. Dip into white melting chocolate (xii).

MAKES 26-40

Raspberry Cheesecake

Raspberry Cheesecake

1 box white cake mix

3 eggs

1 tsp. raspberry extract

1 cup milk

MIX TOGETHER cake mix, eggs, raspberry extract, and milk. Batter will be thick. Pour into a greased 9x13 baking pan. Bake at 350 degrees for 28–32 minutes or until cake springs back when lightly touched. Remove from oven and cool completely. Crumble cake into small, even pieces, placing crumbs in a large bowl.

ADD

8 oz. cream cheese, softened

⅓ cup fresh raspberries, mashed (You can also use frozen raspberries, thawed and squeezed dry.)

WITH THE BACK of a spoon, mix together cake crumbles with other ingredients until a thick dough consistency forms. Shape into evenly sized cake bites (xi) and cool 1–2 hours in the refrigerator, or 20 minutes in the freezer. Dip into white melting chocolate (xii). Top with crushed graham crackers if desired.

MAKES 26-40

Pink Lemonade

This is a girly cake bite, perfect for a girls' night in, baby shower, or wedding shower. Or a get-well or hope-you-feel-better cake bite.

1 box white cake mix

½ cup pink lemonade concentrate, thawed

½ oz. liquid red food coloring

2 eggs

¾ cup milk

2 Tbsp. flour

MIX TOGETHER cake mix, pink lemonade concentrate, red food coloring, eggs, milk, and flour. Batter will be thick. Pour into a greased 9×13 baking pan. Bake at 350 degrees for 28–32 minutes or until cake springs back when lightly touched. Remove from oven and cool completely. Crumble cake into small, even pieces, placing crumbs in a large bowl.

MAKES 26–40

ADD

1 cup Lemon Buttercream Frosting (p)

WITH THE BACK of a spoon, mix together cake crumbles with frosting until a thick dough consistency forms. Shape into evenly sized cake bites (xi) and cool 1–2 hours in the refrigerator, or 20 minutes in the freezer. Dip into white or pink melting chocolate (xii). Top with pink sprinkles or edible pink glitter.

Very Vanilla

Sometimes the best flavors are the most simple.

1 box French vanilla cake mix

1 tsp. vanilla extract

3 eggs

¾ cup half-and-half

MIX TOGETHER cake mix, vanilla extract, eggs, and half-and-half. Batter will be thick. Pour into a greased 9x13 baking pan. Bake at 350 degrees for 28–32 minutes or until cake springs back when lightly touched. Remove from oven and cool completely. Crumble cake into small, even pieces, placing crumbs in a large bowl.

ADD

1 cup Vanilla Buttercream Frosting (125)

WITH THE BACK of a spoon, mix together cake crumbles with frosting until a thick dough consistency forms. Shape into evenly sized cake bites (xi) and cool 1–2 hours in the refrigerator, or 20 minutes in the freezer. Dip into white melting chocolate (xii).

MAKES 26-40

Orange Roll

Orange Roll

Hot, chewy, sweet orange rolls. How do I love thee? Let me count the ways! I eat you for breakfast, snack, lunch, snack, dinner, and dessert!

1 box yellow cake mix

2 Tbsp. grated orange zest

2 Tbsp. orange juice concentrate, thawed

¾ cup half-and-half

2 eggs

2 Tbsp. flour

MIX TOGETHER cake mix, grated orange zest, orange juice concentrate, half-and-half, eggs, and flour. Batter will be thick. Pour into a greased 9x13 baking pan. Bake at 350 degrees for 28–32 minutes or until cake springs back when lightly touched. Remove from oven and cool completely.

ADD

1 cup Vanilla Buttercream Frosting (125)

1 tsp. orange extract.

MAKES 26-40

WITH THE BACK of a spoon, mix together cake crumbles with other ingredients until a thick dough consistency forms. Shape into evenly sized cake bites (xi) and cool 1–2 hours in the refrigerator, or 20 minutes in the freezer. Dip into white melting chocolate (xii).

Strawberry Shortcake

This recipe needs no introduction.

1 box white cake mix

3 eggs

1 tsp. sea or kosher salt

¾ cup half-and-half

MIX TOGETHER cake mix, eggs, salt, and half-and-half. Batter will be thick. Pour into a greased 9x13 baking pan. Bake at 350 degrees for 28–32 minutes or until cake springs back when lightly touched. Remove from oven and cool completely. Crumble cake into small, even pieces, placing crumbs in a large bowl.

ADD

⅓ cup fresh strawberries, mashed (You can also use frozen strawberries, drained and squeezed dry.)

¾ cup Vanilla Buttercream Frosting (125)

MAKES 26-40

WITH THE BACK of a spoon, mix together cake crumbles with other ingredients until a thick dough consistency forms. Shape into evenly sized cake bites (xi) and cool 1–2 hours in the refrigerator, or 20 minutes in the freezer. Dip into white melting chocolate (xii).

Orange Creamsicle

I am beginning to think that I love summer and its treats. I really don't hate the winter. . . . I think.

1 box yellow cake mix

1 tsp. orange extract

3 eggs

¾ cup milk

MIX TOGETHER cake mix, orange extract, eggs, milk, and orange zest. Batter will be thick. Pour into a greased 9x13 baking pan. Bake at 350 degrees for 28–32 minutes or until cake springs back when lightly touched. Remove from oven and cool completely. Crumble cake into small, even pieces, placing crumbs in a large bowl.

ADD

8 oz. cream cheese, softened

¼ cup Vanilla Buttercream Frosting (125)

WITH THE BACK of a spoon, mix together cake crumbles with other ingredients until a thick dough consistency forms. Shape into evenly sized cake bites (xi) and cool 1–2 hours in the refrigerator, or 20 minutes in the freezer. Dip into white melting chocolate (xii).

MAKES 26-40

Good Ole PB & J

Good Ole PB & J

There are some days when I make lunch for the kids—and I join them for a good ole P B & J sandwich and savor the memories from my childhood.

1 box white or yellow cake mix

½ cup peanut butter

3 eggs

¾ cup half-and-half

1 tsp. vanilla extract

MIX TOGETHER cake mix, peanut butter, eggs, half-and-half, and vanilla extract. Batter will be thick. Pour into a greased 9x13 baking pan. Bake at 350 degrees for 28–32 minutes or until cake springs back when lightly touched. Remove from oven and cool completely. Crumble cake into small, even pieces, placing crumbs in a large bowl.

ADD

¾ cup Peanut Butter Frosting (136)

⅓ cup fresh raspberries or strawberries, mashed

(You can also use frozen berries, thawed and squeezed dry.)

MAKES 26–40

WITH THE BACK of a spoon, mix together cake crumbles with other ingredients until a thick dough consistency forms. Shape into evenly sized cake bites (xi) and cool 1–2 hours in the refrigerator, or 20 minutes in the freezer. Dip into white or dark melting chocolate (xii).

Banana Foster

1 box yellow cake mix

2 bananas, mashed

3 eggs

¾ cup milk

1 tsp. cinnamon

1 tsp. rum extract or 2 Tbsp. dark rum

MIX TOGETHER cake mix, mashed bananas, eggs, milk, cinnamon, and rum. Batter will be thick. Pour into a greased 9x13 baking pan. Bake at 350 degrees for 28–32 minutes or until cake springs back when lightly touched. Remove from oven and cool completely.

ADD

1 cup Rum Buttercream Frosting

WITH THE BACK of a spoon, mix together cake crumbles with frosting until a thick dough consistency forms. Shape into evenly sized cake bites (xi) and cool 1–2 hours in the refrigerator, or 20 minutes in the freezer. Dip into white melting chocolate (xii).

MAKES 26-40

Blackberries and Cream

1 box white cake mix

3 eggs

1 tsp. vanilla extract

¾ half-and-half

MIX TOGETHER cake mix, eggs, vanilla, and half-and-half. Batter will be thick. Pour into a greased 9x13 baking pan. Bake at 350 degrees for 28–32 minutes or until cake springs back when lightly touched. Remove from oven and cool completely. Crumble cake into small, even pieces, placing crumbs in a large bowl.

ADD

⅓ cup fresh blackberries, mashed (You can also use frozen blackberries, thawed and squeezed dry.)

¾ cup Vanilla Buttercream Frosting (125)

WITH THE BACK of a spoon, mix together cake crumbles with other ingredients until a thick dough consistency forms. Shape into evenly sized cake bites (xi) and cool 1–2 hours in the refrigerator, or 20 minutes in the freezer. Dip into white melting chocolate (xii).

MAKES 26-40

Cherry Limeade

Cherry Limeade

My kids have a love for a local fast food place. They call it the "apple store." I can't seem to understand why, unless they think the cherry limeade has apples in it. Here's to the best cherry limeade in the world!

1 box white cake mix

1 tsp. cherry flavoring

3 eggs

¾ half-and-half

MIX TOGETHER cake mix, red food coloring, cherry flavoring, eggs, and half-and-half. Batter will be thick. Pour into a greased 9x13 baking pan. Bake at 350 degrees for 28–32 minutes or until cake springs back when lightly touched. Remove from oven and cool completely. Crumble cake into small, even pieces, placing crumbs in a large bowl.

ADD

¾ cup Lime Buttercream Frosting (130)

2 Tbsp. grated lime zest

1 oz. red food coloring, or 2 Tbsp. beet juice

⅓ cup diced maraschino cherries, rinsed and drained

MAKES 26–40

WITH THE BACK of a spoon, mix together cake crumbles with other ingredients until a thick dough consistency forms. Shape into evenly sized cake bites (xi) and cool 1–2 hours in the refrigerator, or 20 minutes in the freezer. Dip into white or red melting chocolate (xii).

Sour Cream Blueberry

Sour cream + Blueberries+ Cake Bites= Priceless

1 box white cake mix

1 cup sour cream

3 eggs

¾ cup milk

1 tsp. vanilla extract

MIX TOGETHER cake mix, sour cream, eggs, milk, and vanilla extract. Batter will be thick. Pour into a greased 9x13 baking pan. Bake at 350 degrees for 28–32 minutes or until cake springs back when lightly touched. Remove from oven and cool completely.

ADD

¾ cup Vanilla Buttercream Frosting (125)

½ cup chopped dried blueberries

⅓ cup sour cream

MAKES 26-40

WITH THE BACK of a spoon, mix together cake crumbles with other ingredients until a thick dough consistency forms. Shape into evenly sized cake bites (xi) and cool 1–2 hours in the refrigerator, or 20 minutes in the freezer. Dip into white melting chocolate (xii).

Sour Cream Raspberry

Well, all things fruity are a treat for me. I love picking fresh raspberries. Eat as you go, that is my motto. And enjoy the harvest. . . . That is my other motto.

1 box white cake mix

1 cup sour cream

3 eggs

¾ cup milk

1 tsp. vanilla extract

MIX TOGETHER cake mix, sour cream, eggs, milk, and vanilla extract. Batter will be thick. Pour into a greased 9x13 baking pan. Bake at 350 degrees for 28–32 minutes or until cake springs back when lightly touched. Remove from oven and cool completely. Crumble cake into small, even pieces, placing crumbs in a large bowl.

ADD

¾ cup Raspberry Buttercream Frosting (141)

½ cup fresh raspberries, mashed (You can also use frozen raspberries, thawed and squeezed dry.)

⅓ cup sour cream

MAKES 26–40

WITH THE BACK of a spoon, mix together cake crumbles with other ingredients until a thick dough consistency forms. Shape into evenly sized cake bites (xi) and cool 1–2 hours in the refrigerator, or 20 minutes in the freezer. Dip into white melting chocolate (xii).

Caramel Apple

Caramel Apple

One is not enough. Go ahead and have two if you'd like. Maybe even three. I won't tell anyone.

1 box spice cake mix

3 eggs

¼ cup oil

¾ cup applesauce

½ cup half-and-half

1 tsp. vanilla extract

1 tsp. cinnamon

MIX TOGETHER cake mix, eggs, oil, applesauce, half-and-half, vanilla extract, and cinnamon. Batter will be thick. Pour into a greased 9x13 baking pan. Bake at 350 degrees for 28–32 minutes or until cake springs back when lightly touched. Remove from oven and cool completely. Crumble cake into small, even pieces, placing crumbs in a large bowl.

ADD

½ cup Caramel Cream Frosting (128)

½ cup caramel sauce (I love Mrs. Richardson's)

WITH THE BACK of a spoon, mix together cake crumbles with other ingredients until a thick dough consistency forms. Shape into evenly sized cake bites (xi) and cool 1–2 hours in the refrigerator, or 20 minutes in the freezer. Drizzle with additional caramel sauce. Then sprinkle with cinnamon and sugar, chopped nuts, or white chocolate. Be creative!

MAKES 26-40

Lemon Coconut

This recipe is for my friend Ann. While brainstorming about possible combinations, she came up with this one. It's fantastic. . . . The flavors melt in your mouth. Ann, you are an inspiration. Thanks for being my friend.

1 box lemon cake mix

3 eggs

¾ cup milk

1 tsp. lemon extract

MIX TOGETHER cake mix, eggs, milk, and lemon extract. Batter will be thick. Pour into a greased 9x13 baking pan. Bake at 350 degrees for 28–32 minutes, until cake springs back when lightly touched. Remove from oven and cool completely.

ADD

1 cup Coconut Buttercream Frosting (133)

½ cup shredded coconut

MAKES 26-40

WITH THE BACK of a spoon, mix together cake crumbles with other ingredients until a thick dough consistency forms. Shape into evenly sized cake bites (xi) and cool 1–2 hours in the refrigerator, or 20 minutes in the freezer. Dip into white melting chocolate (xii). Top with shredded coconut.

The Sweetness of Chocolate

Chocolate Peanut Butter Cup

Chocolate Peanut Butter Cup

I have certain food pleasures that I allow myself to indulge in from time to time. Chocolate peanut butter cups are one of those pleasures. It's hard for me to eat only one . . . especially in a cake bite.

1 box dark chocolate cake mix

3 eggs

1 tsp. vanilla extract

¾ cup half-and-half

MIX TOGETHER cake mix, eggs, vanilla extract, and half-and-half. Batter will be thick. Pour into a greased 9x13 baking pan. Bake at 350 degrees for 28–32 minutes or until cake springs back when lightly touched. Remove from oven and cool completely. Crumble cake into small, even pieces, placing crumbs in a large bowl.

ADD

1 cup Chocolate Buttercream Frosting (126) or 1 cup Peanut Butter Frosting (136)

3 pkgs. (1.5 oz) regular-size peanut butter cups, unwrapped and coarsely chopped

MAKES 26–40

WITH THE BACK of a spoon, mix together cake crumbles with other ingredients until a thick dough consistency forms. Shape into evenly sized cake bites (xi) and cool 1–2 hours in the refrigerator, or 20 minutes in the freezer. Dip into white melting chocolate (xii). Drizzle with melted chocolate and/or chopped peanuts.

White Chocolate Macadamia

White Chocolate Macadamia

One of my all-time favorite cookies is white chocolate macadamia—I may have to bake some up right now.

1 box white cake mix

3 eggs

1 tsp. vanilla extract

1 cup half-and-half

MIX TOGETHER cake mix, eggs, vanilla extract, and half-and-half. Batter will be thick. Pour into a greased 9x13 baking pan. Bake at 350 degrees for 28–32 minutes or until cake springs back when lightly touched. Remove from oven and cool completely. Crumble cake into small, even pieces, placing crumbs in a large bowl.

ADD

⅓ cup macadamia nuts, chopped

⅓ cup white chocolate, chopped

¾ cup Vanilla Buttercream Frosting (125)

MAKES 26–40

WITH THE BACK of a spoon, mix together cake crumbles with other ingredients until a thick dough consistency forms. Shape into evenly sized cake bites (xi) and cool 1–2 hours in the refrigerator, or 20 minutes in the freezer. Dip into white melting chocolate (xii). Drizzle with melted chocolate and/or chopped macadamia nuts.

Chocolate Caramel Toffee

Ever wonder what to do when a batch of toffee doesn't turn out? Well, save the crumbs or several pieces and use them to make this delicious mouth-watering cake bite.

1 box dark chocolate cake mix

3 eggs

1 tsp. vanilla extract

1 cup milk

MIX TOGETHER cake mix, eggs, vanilla extract, and milk. Batter will be thick. Pour into a greased 9x13 baking pan. Bake at 350 degrees for 28–32 minutes or until cake springs back when lightly touched. Remove from oven and cool completely. Crumble cake into small, even pieces, placing crumbs in a large bowl.

ADD

1 cup Caramel Cream Frosting (128) or 1 cup Chocolate Buttercream Frosting (126)

½ cup crushed toffee pieces

MAKES 26-40

WITH THE BACK of a spoon, mix together cake crumbles with other ingredients until a thick dough consistency forms. Shape into evenly sized cake bites (xi) and cool 1–2 hours in the refrigerator, or 20 minutes in the freezer. Dip into dark melting chocolate (xii). Drizzle with melted chocolate and crushed toffee pieces.

Dark Chocolate Truffle

Chocolate is like a drug for some people. Eating the smallest portion calms fears, takes away pain, and eases the slightest discomforts in life. I believe chocolate is a form of therapy—and it's certainly cheaper than shopping!

1 box dark chocolate cake mix

3 eggs

1 cup milk

1 tsp. vanilla extract

MIX TOGETHER cake mix, eggs, milk, and vanilla extract. Batter will be thick. Pour into a greased 9x13 baking pan. Bake at 350 degrees for 28–32 minutes or until cake springs back when lightly touched. Remove from oven and cool completely. Crumble cake into small, even pieces, placing crumbs in a large bowl.

ADD

1 cup Chocolate Ganache (124), room temperature

½ cup mini chocolate chips

WITH THE BACK of a spoon, mix together cake crumbles with other ingredients until a thick dough consistency forms. Shape into evenly sized cake bites (xi) and cool 1–2 hours in the refrigerator, or 20 minutes in the freezer. Dip into dark melting chocolate (xii). Sprinkle with mini chocolate chips or drizzle with dark chocolate.

MAKES 26-40

Cherry Cordial

Cherry Cordial

There are no words to describe the happiness my taste buds feel when I eat chocolate and cherries together. Yum!

1 box chocolate cake mix

1 cup half-and-half

1 tsp. cherry extract

3 eggs

MIX TOGETHER cake mix, half-and-half, cherry extract, and eggs. Batter will be thick. Pour into a greased 9x13 baking pan. Bake at 350 degrees for 28–32 minutes or until cake springs back when lightly touched. Remove from oven and cool completely. Crumble cake into small, even pieces, placing crumbs in a large bowl.

ADD

¾ cup Chocolate Buttercream Frosting (126)

½ cup chopped maraschino cherries, rinsed, drained, and laid out on a paper towel to dry

WITH THE BACK of a spoon, mix together cake crumbles with other ingredients until a thick dough consistency forms. Shape into evenly sized cake bites (xi) and cool 1–2 hours in the refrigerator, or 20 minutes in the freezer. Dip into dark melting chocolate (xii). Drizzle with melted chocolate.

MAKES 26-40

Mexican Chocolate Chili

For my book release party for 101 Gourmet Cupcakes, I had a cupcake contest. The winner made this fantastic chocolate and chili cupcake, reminiscent of Mayan chocolate treats. . . . Stephenie, your cupcake is the perfect inspiration for this cake bite.

1 box chocolate cake mix

3 eggs

1 cup milk

1 tsp. cayenne pepper

1 Tbsp. cinnamon

1 tsp. vanilla extract

MIX TOGETHER cake mix, eggs, milk, cayenne pepper, cinnamon, and vanilla extract. Batter will be thick. Pour into a greased 9x13 baking pan. Bake at 350 degrees for 28–32 minutes or until cake springs back when lightly touched. Remove from oven and cool completely. Crumble cake into small, even pieces, placing crumbs in a large bowl.

ADD
1 cup Chocolate Ganache (124)

MAKES 26–40

WITH THE BACK of a spoon, mix together cake crumbles with ganache until a thick dough consistency forms. Shape into evenly sized cake bites (xi) and cool 1–2 hours in the refrigerator, or 20 minutes in the freezer. Dip into dark melting chocolate (xii). Drizzle with melted chocolate and sprinkle with cayenne pepper if you dare.

Even More S'more

The mere thought of marshmallow, chocolate, and graham crackers mixed together makes me smile from ear to ear.

1 box German chocolate cake mix

3 eggs

1 tsp. vanilla extract

¾ cup milk

MIX TOGETHER cake mix, eggs, vanilla extract, and milk. Batter will be thick. Pour into a greased 9x13 baking pan. Bake at 350 degrees for 28–32 minutes or until cake springs back when lightly touched. Remove from oven and cool completely. Crumble cake into small, even pieces, placing crumbs in a large bowl.

ADD

½ cup marshmallow cream

½ cup Chocolate Buttercream Frosting (126)

¼ cup crushed graham crackers

¼ cup mini chocolate chips

MAKES 26–40

WITH THE BACK of a spoon, mix together cake crumbles with other ingredients until a thick dough consistency forms. Shape into evenly sized cake bites (xi) and cool 1–2 hours in the refrigerator, or 20 minutes in the freezer. Dip into dark melting chocolate (xii). Drizzle with melted chocolate and/or crushed graham crackers.

Mint Brownie

Mint Brownie

Parts of Utah are famous for their mint brownies. . . . And I won't say which parts. This cake bite brings all the flavors together in a little bite.

1 box chocolate cake mix

3 eggs

1 cup milk

1 tsp. mint extract

MIX TOGETHER cake mix, eggs, milk, and mint extract. Batter will be thick. Pour into a greased 9x13 baking pan. Bake at 350 degrees for 28–32 minutes or until cake springs back when lightly touched. Remove from oven and cool completely. Crumble cake into small, even pieces, placing crumbs in a large bowl.

ADD

1 cup Chocolate Buttercream Frosting (126)

WITH THE BACK of a spoon, mix together cake crumbles with frosting until a thick dough consistency forms. Shape into evenly sized cake bites (xi) and cool 1–2 hours in the refrigerator, or 20 minutes in the freezer. Dip into dark melting chocolate (xii). Drizzle with melted mint chocolate chips (green).

MAKES 26-40

Nanaimo Brownie

There are a few desserts that I am obsessed with—Nanaimo Brownies are one of them. From the moment I first shared this dessert with my husband in Vancouver, I knew they would be a part of my food world. Now I still get excited to make these treats, and even more excited to eat them!

1 box chocolate cake mix

1 tsp. almond extract

3 eggs

1 cup half-and-half

MIX TOGETHER cake mix, almond extract, eggs, and half-and-half. Batter will be thick. Pour into a greased 9x13 baking pan. Bake at 350 degrees for 28–32 minutes or until cake springs back when lightly touched. Remove from oven and cool completely. Crumble cake into small, even pieces, placing crumbs in a large bowl.

ADD

1 cup Custard Cream Frosting (140)

⅓ cup chopped almonds

⅓ cup shredded coconut

MAKES 26–40

WITH THE BACK of a spoon, mix together cake crumbles with other ingredients until a thick dough consistency forms. Shape into evenly sized cake bites (xi) and cool 1–2 hours in the refrigerator, or 20 minutes in the freezer. Dip into dark melting chocolate (xii). Top with graham cracker crumbs if desired.

Cookies and Cream

The best of both world. Dark smooth chocolate with cream. A perfect treat anytime, anywhere.

1 box chocolate cake mix

2 eggs

1 cup milk

1 tsp. vanilla extract

MIX TOGETHER cake mix, eggs, milk, and vanilla extract. Batter will be thick. Pour into a greased 9x13 baking pan. Bake at 350 degrees for 28–32 minutes or until cake springs back when lightly touched. Remove from oven and cool completely. Crumble cake into small, even pieces, placing crumbs in a large bowl. Crumble cake into small, even pieces, placing crumbs in a large bowl.

ADD

1 cup Chocolate Buttercream Frosting (126) or Vanilla Buttercream Frosting (125)

1 cup crushed chocolate sandwich cookies

WITH THE BACK of a spoon, mix together cake crumbles with other ingredients until a thick dough consistency forms. Shape into evenly sized cake bites (xi) and cool 1–2 hours in the refrigerator, or 20 minutes in the freezer. Dip into dark melting chocolate (xii). Top with crushed cookie crumbs.

MAKES 26-40

A Rockier Road

A Rockier Road

I am not crazy. I am not insane (although my family may say otherwise). I like being creative in the kitchen. And when I find a recipe I love, I make it over and over again. For example A Rocky Road cupcake. . . . It was so good, I had to keep going. I couldn't stop at the cupcake alone. I had to make a Rockier Road cake bite. Okay, so maybe I am a little crazy.

1 box dark chocolate or chocolate fudge cake mix

¼ cup finely chopped almonds

3 eggs

1 cup milk

1 tsp. vanilla extract

MIX TOGETHER cake mix, chopped almonds, eggs, milk, and vanilla extract. Batter will be thick. Pour into a greased 9x13 baking pan. Bake at 350 degrees for 28–32 minutes or until cake springs back when lightly touched. Remove from oven and cool completely. Crumble cake into small, even pieces, placing crumbs in a large bowl.

ADD

1 cup Chocolate Buttercream Frosting (126)

1 cup mini marshmallows

MAKES 26–40

WITH THE BACK of a spoon, mix together cake crumbles with other ingredients until a thick dough consistency forms. Shape into evenly sized cake bites (xi) and cool 1–2 hours in the refrigerator, or 20 minutes in the freezer. Dip into dark melting chocolate (xii). Top with almonds (optional).

Chocolate Orange

You know those little chocolate oranges that Santa sometimes leaves in your stocking? Well, I thought, how perfect to make a bite-sized version, full of that same orangey chocolate goodness. Now you can have them year round—not just during the holidays.

1 box chocolate cake mix

3 eggs

3 tsp. orange extract

2 Tbsp. orange zest

1 cup milk

MIX TOGETHER cake mix, eggs, orange extract, orange zest, and milk. Batter will be thick. Pour into a greased 9x13 baking pan. Bake at 350 degrees for 28–32 minutes or until cake springs back when lightly touched. Remove from oven and cool completely. Crumble cake into small, even pieces, placing crumbs in a large bowl.

ADD

1 cup Chocolate Buttercream Frosting (126) plus 1 tsp. Orange extract

2 Tbsp. orange zest

MAKES 26–40

WITH THE BACK of a spoon, mix together cake crumbles with other ingredients until a thick dough consistency forms. Shape into evenly sized cake bites (xi) and cool 1–2 hours in the refrigerator, or 20 minutes in the freezer. Dip into dark melting chocolate (xii).

Grasshopper

A light, refreshing mint flavor with all the favorite ingredients of a traditional grasshopper pie.

1 box chocolate cake mix

3 eggs

1 tsp. mint extract

1 cup milk

MIX TOGETHER cake mix, eggs, mint extract, and milk. Batter will be thick. Pour into a greased 9x13 baking pan. Bake at 350 degrees for 28–32 minutes or until cake springs back when lightly touched. Remove from oven and cool completely. Crumble cake into small, even pieces, placing crumbs in a large bowl.

ADD

½ cup Chocolate Buttercream Frosting (126)

½ cup marshmallow cream

WITH THE BACK back of a spoon, mix together cake crumbles with other ingredients until a thick dough consistency forms. Shape into evenly sized cake bites (xi) and cool 1–2 hours in the refrigerator, or 20 minutes in the freezer. Dip into dark melting chocolate (xii). Top or cover entire cake bite with crushed chocolate sandwich cookies.

MAKES 26-40

White Chocolate Cranberry

White Chocolate Cranberry

Tasty. Simple. Fun. For me, the simple desserts are the best. The desserts you can include your children in making, designing, and creating.

1 box white cake mix

3 eggs

½ tsp. nutmeg

1 cup milk

MIX TOGETHER cake mix, eggs, nutmeg, and milk. Batter will be thick. Pour into a greased 9x13 baking pan. Bake at 350 degrees for 28–32 minutes or until cake springs back when lightly touched. Remove from oven and cool completely. Crumble cake into small, even pieces, placing crumbs in a large bowl.

ADD

1 cup Vanilla Buttercream Frosting (125)

½ cup chopped white chocolate

½ cup dried cranberries (optional)

MAKES 26–40

WITH THE BACK of a spoon, mix together cake crumbles with other ingredients until a thick dough consistency forms. Shape into evenly sized cake bites (xi) and cool 1–2 hours in the refrigerator, or 20 minutes in the freezer. Dip into white melting chocolate (xii). Top with dried cranberries (optional).

Chocolate Cinnamon Zucchini

Are there ever enough zucchini recipes when you need them? If you want to omit the zucchini entirely from this recipe, go ahead. For me it's the best part! I get to be sneaky with the vegetables. . . . "Kids! Who wants a chocolate cake bite for a snack today?"

1 box chocolate cake mix

3 eggs

1 Tbsp. cinnamon

1 cup half-and-half

1 cup grated zucchini

1 tsp. vanilla extract

MIX TOGETHER cake mix, eggs, cinnamon, half-and-half, zucchini, and vanilla extract. Batter will be thick. Pour into a greased 9x13 baking pan. Bake at 350 degrees for 28–32 minutes or until cake springs back when lightly touched. Remove from oven and cool completely. Crumble cake into small, even pieces, placing crumbs in a large bowl.

MAKES 26–40

ADD

1 cup Chocolate Buttercream Frosting (126) or Cinnamon Vanilla Buttercream Frosting (135)

WITH THE BACK of a spoon, mix together cake crumbles with frosting until a thick dough consistency forms. Shape into evenly sized cake bites (xi) and cool 1–2 hours in the refrigerator, or 20 minutes in the freezer. Dip into dark melting chocolate (xii).

Chocolate Bahamas

On a cruise some many years ago, I had the privilege of eating these amazing chocolate balls from heaven. Here is my version in honor of all my cruising buddies from my past—you know who you are. When are we going again? I could use a vacation soon. Very, very soon.

1 dark chocolate cake mix

3 eggs

1 cup milk

1 tsp. rum extract or 2 Tbsp. dark rum

MIX TOGETHER cake mix, eggs, milk, and rum extract. Batter will be thick. Pour into a greased 9x13 baking pan. Bake at 350 degrees for 28–32 minutes or until cake springs back when lightly touched. Remove from oven and cool completely. Crumble cake into small, even pieces, placing crumbs in a large bowl.

ADD

1 cup Chocolate Ganache (124), at room temperature

1 tsp. rum extract or 2 Tbsp. dark rum

WITH THE BACK of a spoon, mix together cake crumbles with other ingredients until a thick dough consistency forms. Shape into evenly sized cake bites (xi) and cool 1–2 hours in the refrigerator, or 20 minutes in the freezer. Dip into dark melting chocolate (xii).

MAKES 26–40

Chocolate Hazelnut

Chocolate Hazelnut

I did it! After much begging and pleading from my daughter, I made a cake bite with Nutella. Yes, all Nutella fans out there will simply love, love, love this cake bite. Just like my daughter does.

1 dark chocolate cake mix

3 eggs

1 cup milk

1 tsp. vanilla extract

MIX TOGETHER cake mix, eggs, milk, and vanilla extract. Batter will be thick. Pour into a greased 9x13 baking pan. Bake at 350 degrees for 28–32 minutes or until cake springs back when lightly touched. Remove from oven and cool completely. Crumble cake into small, even pieces, placing crumbs in a large bowl.

ADD

1 cup Nutella

½ cup mini semi-sweet chocolate chips

WITH THE BACK of a spoon, mix together cake crumbles with other ingredients until a thick dough consistency forms. Shape into evenly sized cake bites (xi) and cool 1–2 hours in the refrigerator, or 20 minutes in the freezer. Dip into dark melting chocolate (xii). Top with chopped hazelnuts if desired. You can even melt some Nutella in the microwave for 10–15 seconds and drizzle your cake bite with it—double yum.

MAKES 26-40

German Chocolate

A classic cake, rolled into a bite size piece of heaven. I'm filled with delight! I may even need some therapy to overcome my love of chocolate.

1 box German chocolate cake mix

3 eggs

1 cup milk

1 tsp. vanilla extract

MIX TOGETHER cake mix, eggs, milk, and vanilla extract. Batter will be thick. Pour into a greased 9x13 baking pan. Bake at 350 degrees for 28–32 minutes or until cake springs back when lightly touched. Remove from oven and cool completely. Crumble cake into small, even pieces, placing crumbs in a large bowl.

ADD

½ cup Caramel Cream Frosting (128)

½ cup toasted coconut

⅓ cup caramel sauce

MAKES 26–40

WITH THE BACK of a spoon, mix together cake crumbles with other ingredients until a thick dough consistency forms. Shape into evenly sized cake bites (xi) and cool 1–2 hours in the refrigerator, or 20 minutes in the freezer. Dip into dark melting chocolate (xii). Top with toasted coconut if desired.

Chocolate Raspberry Brownie

The title says more about this cake bite than I ever could. Again, shall we? Chocolate. Raspberry. Brownie.

1 box dark chocolate cake mix

3 eggs

¾ cup milk

¼ cup vegetable oil

1 tsp. vanilla extract

MIX TOGETHER cake mix, eggs, milk, vegetable oil, and vanilla extract. Batter will be thick. Pour into a greased 9x13 baking pan. Bake at 350 degrees for 28–32 minutes or until cake springs back when lightly touched. Remove from oven and cool completely. Crumble cake into small, even pieces, placing crumbs in a large bowl.

ADD

1 cup Raspberry Buttercream Frosting (141)

½ cup chopped dried or dehydrated raspberries

¼ cup mini semi-sweet chocolate chips

MAKES 26–40

WITH THE BACK of a spoon, mix together cake crumbles with other ingredients until a thick dough consistency forms. Shape into evenly sized cake bites (xi) and cool 1–2 hours in the refrigerator, or 20 minutes in the freezer. Dip into dark melting chocolate (xii).

Chocolate Chip Cookie

Chocolate Chip Cookie

With all the baking I have done the last, well, my entire life, I asked my seven-year-old son, "What's your all-time favorite treat I've baked for you?" Without any hesitation he said, "Chocolate chip cookies."

1 box yellow cake mix

3 eggs

¾ cup milk

¼ cup oil

1 tsp. vanilla extract

MIX TOGETHER cake mix, eggs, milk, vegetable oil, and vanilla extract. Batter will be thick. Pour into a greased 9x13 baking pan. Bake at 350 degrees for 28–32 minutes or until cake springs back when lightly touched. Remove from oven and cool completely. Crumble cake into small, even pieces, placing crumbs in a large bowl.

ADD

¾ cup Vanilla Buttercream Frosting (125)

½ cup mini semi-sweet chocolate chips (optional)

WITH THE BACK of a spoon, mix together cake crumbles with other ingredients until a thick dough consistency forms. Shape into evenly sized cake bites (xi) and cool 1–2 hours in the refrigerator, or 20 minutes in the freezer. Dip into white or dark melting chocolate (xii). Top with mini semi-sweet chocolate chips (optional).

MAKES 26-40

Chocolate Cream Pie

Chocolate Cream Pie

Seriously, I know. This recipe is the very last one that I wrote for this book. I think I saved the best for last. Yummylicious.

1 box chocolate cake mix

3 eggs

1 cup milk

1 tsp. vanilla extract

MIX TOGETHER cake mix, eggs, milk, and vanilla extract. Batter will be thick. Pour into a greased 9x13 baking pan. Bake at 350 degrees for 28–32 minutes or until cake springs back when lightly touched. Remove from oven and cool completely. Crumble cake into small, even pieces, placing crumbs in a large bowl.

ADD

8 oz. cream cheese softened

¼ cup Chocolate Buttercream Frosting (126)

WITH THE BACK of a spoon, mix together cake crumbles with other ingredients until a thick dough consistency forms. Shape into evenly sized cake bites (xi) and cool 1–2 hours in the refrigerator, or 20 minutes in the freezer. Dip into dark melting chocolate (xii).

MAKES 26-40

Chocolate Almond

I love to bake, love to cook, and love to eat what I make in the kitchen, especially these chocolate almond cake bites. Now if I could only be 10 lbs. thinner, the world would be a perfect place. (Ha ha!)

1 box chocolate cake mix

1 tsp. almond extract

1 cup milk

3 eggs

¼ cup finely chopped almonds

MIX TOGETHER cake mix, almond extract, milk, eggs, and chopped almonds. Batter will be thick. Pour into a greased 9x13 baking pan. Bake at 350 degrees for 28–32 minutes or until cake springs back when lightly touched. Remove from oven and cool completely. Crumble cake into small, even pieces, placing crumbs in a large bowl.

ADD

1 cup Chocolate Buttercream Frosting (126)

MAKES 26-40

WITH THE BACK of a spoon, mix together cake crumbles with frosting until a thick dough consistency forms. Shape into evenly sized cake bites (xi) and cool 1–2 hours in the refrigerator, or 20 minutes in the freezer. Dip into dark melting chocolate (xii). Top with finely chopped almonds if desired.

Holiday Treats

Egg Nog

Egg Nog

'Tis the season . . . egg nog cupcakes, egg nog waffles, egg nog cake bites . . . need I say more? These little bites are a delight to serve on your next holiday platter.

1 box yellow cake mix

3 eggs

1 cup half-and-half

1 tsp. cinnamon

½ tsp. nutmeg

½ tsp. rum extract

MIX TOGETHER cake mix, eggs, half-and-half, cinnamon, nutmeg, and rum extract. Batter will be thick. Pour into a greased 9x13 baking pan. Bake at 350 degrees for 28–32 minutes or until cake springs back when lightly touched. Remove from oven and cool completely. Crumble cake into small, even pieces, placing crumbs in a large bowl.

ADD

1 cup Vanilla Buttercream Frosting (125)

1 tsp. rum extract or 2 Tbsp. dark rum

MAKES 26–40

WITH THE BACK of a spoon, mix together cake crumbles with other ingredients until a thick dough consistency forms. Shape into evenly sized cake bites (xi) and cool 1–2 hours in the refrigerator, or 20 minutes in the freezer. Dip into white melting chocolate (xii). Sprinkle with nutmeg if desired.

Pumpkin Pie

One of the best things about Thanksgiving is pumpkin pie. I just love this cake bite so much. . . . What makes it even better, is a dollop of whipped cream served on the side.

1 box spice cake mix

1 cup pumpkin puree

1 tsp. pumpkin pie spice

3 eggs

½ cup half-and-half

MIX TOGETHER cake mix, pumpkin puree, pumpkin pie spice, eggs, and half-and-half. Batter will be thick. Pour into a greased 9×13 baking pan. Bake at 350 degrees for 28–32 minutes or until cake springs back when lightly touched. Remove from oven and cool completely. Crumble cake into small, even pieces, placing crumbs in a large bowl.

ADD

¾ cup Cinnamon Spice Buttercream Frosting

¼ cup pumpkin puree

MAKES 26–40

WITH THE BACK of a spoon, mix together cake crumbles with other ingredients until a thick dough consistency forms. Shape into evenly sized cake bites (xi) and cool 1–2 hours in the refrigerator, or 20 minutes in the freezer. Dip into white or dark melting chocolate (xii). Serve with a dollop of whipped cream for a tasty treat.

American Apple Pie

What is your favorite American food tradition? All-American apple pie, perhaps? This cake bite is a tribute for the great love affair of food we Americans have had for centuries.

1 box spice cake mix

1 cup applesauce

3 eggs

¾ cup milk

1 tsp. vanilla extract

MIX TOGETHER cake mix, applesauce, eggs, milk, and vanilla extract. Batter will be thick. Pour into a greased 9x13 baking pan. Bake at 350 degrees for 28–32 minutes or until cake springs back when lightly touched. Remove from oven and cool completely. Crumble cake into small, even pieces, placing crumbs in a large bowl.

ADD

½ cup Cinnamon Vanilla Buttercream Frosting (135)

½ cup apple pie filling (make sure apple chunks are finely diced)

WITH THE BACK of a spoon, mix together cake crumbles with other ingredients until a thick dough consistency forms. Shape into evenly sized cake bites (xi) and cool 1–2 hours in the refrigerator, or 20 minutes in the freezer. Dip into white melting chocolate (xii).

MAKES 26-40

Sweet Potato Pie

Sweet Potato Pie

Southern sweet potato pie is a legend . . . and if you haven't tried sweet potatoes in a decadent dessert, seize the moment. Take advantage of this easy and very "sweet" recipe.

1 box spice cake mix

1 cup cooked, mashed sweet potatoes

3 eggs

1 cup milk

1 tsp. black pepper (trust me, please)

1 tsp. vanilla extract

½ tsp. nutmeg

MIX TOGETHER cake mix, sweet potatoes, eggs, milk, pepper, vanilla extract, and nutmeg. Batter will be thick. Pour into a greased 9x13 baking pan. Bake at 350 degrees for 28–32 minutes or until cake springs back when lightly touched. Remove from oven and cool completely. Crumble cake into small, even pieces, placing crumbs in a large bowl.

ADD

¾ cup Vanilla Buttercream Frosting (125)

¼ cup cooked, mashed sweet potatoes

fresh cracked pepper (optional)

MAKES 26-40

WITH THE BACK of a spoon, mix together cake crumbles with frosting and sweet potatoes until a thick dough consistency forms. Shape into evenly sized cake bites (xi) and cool 1–2 hours in the refrigerator, or 20 minutes in the freezer. Dip into white melting chocolate (xii). You can, if you are daring, sprinkle with fresh cracked pepper on top (optional).

Pralines and Cream

I must be in a Southern desserts theme . . . or something. But this happens to be one of my absolute favorite cake bites. Of ALL time.

1 box butter pecan cake mix

½ cup finely chopped pecans

3 eggs

1 tsp. vanilla extract

1 cup half-and-half

MIX TOGETHER cake mix, pecans, eggs, vanilla extract, and half-and-half. Batter will be thick. Pour into a greased 9x13 baking pan. Bake at 350 degrees for 28–32 minutes or until cake springs back when lightly touched. Remove from oven and cool completely. Crumble cake into small, even pieces, placing crumbs in a large bowl.

MAKES 26–40

ADD

¾ cup Vanilla Buttercream Frosting (125)

¼ cup caramel sauce (I love Mrs. Richardson's)

½ cup chopped pecans

WITH THE BACK of a spoon, mix together cake crumbles with other ingredients until a thick dough consistency forms. Shape into evenly sized cake bites (xi) and cool 1–2 hours in the refrigerator, or 20 minutes in the freezer. Dip into white melting chocolate (xii).

Harvest Pumpkin

I am always so excited for autumn. . . . The colors of the leaves, the crisp morning air, the great flavors of baking and cooking coming from my kitchen—including this recipe.

1 box spice cake mix

1 cup pumpkin puree

3 eggs

¾ cup milk

MIX TOGETHER cake mix, pumpkin puree, eggs, and milk. Batter will be thick. Pour into a greased 9x13 baking pan. Bake at 350 degrees for 28–32 minutes or until cake springs back when lightly touched. Remove from oven and cool completely. Crumble cake into small, even pieces, placing crumbs in a large bowl.

ADD

¾ cup Vanilla Buttercream Frosting (125)

½ cup pumpkin puree

½ cup finely chopped butterscotch chips

WITH THE BACK of a spoon, mix together cake crumbles with other ingredients until a thick dough consistency forms. Shape into evenly sized cake bites (xi) and cool 1–2 hours in the refrigerator, or 20 minutes in the freezer. Dip into dark melting chocolate (xii).

MAKES 26-40

Root Beer Float

Root Beer Float

Pure root beer flavor with the added whimsy of cake bites. Perfect.

1 box white cake mix

1 tsp. vanilla extract

1 cup milk

3 eggs

2 Tbsp. root beer flavoring

MIX TOGETHER cake mix, vanilla extract, milk, eggs, and root beer flavoring. Batter will be thick. Pour into a greased 9x13 baking pan. Bake at 350 degrees for 28–32 minutes or until cake springs back when lightly touched. Remove from oven and cool completely. Crumble cake into small, even pieces, placing crumbs in a large bowl.

ADD

1 cup Root Beer Buttercream Frosting (127)

WITH THE BACK of a spoon, mix together cake crumbles with frosting until a thick dough consistency forms. Shape into evenly sized cake bites (xi) and cool 1–2 hours in the refrigerator, or 20 minutes in the freezer. Dip into white melting chocolate (xii).

MAKES 26-40

Browned Butter

Have you ever tasted browned butter frosting? Now is your chance. Its nutty, earthy flavor is out-of-this-world delicious.

1 box butter cake mix

½ cup room temperature browned butter (recipe below)

½ cup milk

3 eggs

MIX TOGETHER cake mix, browned butter, milk, and eggs. Batter will be thick. Pour into a greased 9x13 baking pan. Bake at 350 degrees for 28–32 minutes or until cake springs back when lightly touched. Remove from oven and cool completely. Crumble cake into small, even pieces, placing crumbs in a large bowl.

ADD

1 cup Browned Butter Frosting (134)

WITH THE BACK of a spoon, mix together cake crumbles with frosting until a thick dough consistency forms. Shape into evenly sized cake bites (xi) and cool 1–2 hours in the refrigerator, or 20 minutes in the freezer. Dip into white melting chocolate (xii).

MAKES 26-40

BROWNED BUTTER RECIPE: Place 1 stick or ½ cup of butter in a medium skillet. Heat skillet and butter over medium heat until melted and bubbly. You will start to see light golden flecks of butter. Stir occasionally while watching the butter closely. (Now is not the time to change a load of laundry.) Remove from heat once dark golden flecks appear. You will be able to smell the "burned butter" or "nutty" smell. Cool to room temperature before using.

White Chocolate Caramel Cheesecake

A gourmet taste without the typical gourmet baking time is amazing in and of itself. But when it comes in the form of a gourmet cake bite—so simple yet elegant—it's divine.

1 box white cake mix

3 eggs

1 tsp. vanilla extract

1 cup milk

MIX TOGETHER cake mix, eggs, vanilla extract, and milk. Batter will be thick. Pour into a greased 9x13 baking pan. Bake at 350 degrees for 28–32 minutes or until cake springs back when lightly touched. Remove from oven and cool completely. Crumble cake into small, even pieces, placing crumbs in a large bowl.

ADD

8 oz. cream cheese, softened

½ cup chopped white chocolate

¼ cup caramel sauce, optional (again, I love Mrs. Richardson's)

MAKES 26-40

WITH THE BACK of a spoon, mix together cake crumbles with other ingredients until a thick dough consistency forms. Shape into evenly sized cake bites (xi) and cool 1–2 hours in the refrigerator, or 20 minutes in the freezer. Dip into white melting chocolate (xii). Drizzle with caramel sauce (optional).

Southern Red Velvet

Southern Red Velvet

These cake bites are absolutely beautiful, sinfully tasty, and moist.

HINT: While rolling these cake bites, be sure to wear gloves, or your hands will be as red as these little bites.

1 box red velvet cake mix

3 eggs

1 cup half-and-half

1 tsp. vanilla extract

½ cup sour cream

MIX TOGETHER cake mix, eggs, half-and-half, vanilla extract, and sour cream. Batter will be thick. Pour into a greased 9x13 baking pan. Bake at 350 degrees for 28–32 minutes or until cake springs back when lightly touched. Remove from oven and cool completely. Crumble cake into small, even pieces, placing crumbs in a large bowl.

ADD

8 oz. cream cheese, softened

½ cup Vanilla Buttercream Frosting (125)

WITH THE BACK of a spoon, mix together cake crumbles with other ingredients until a thick dough consistency forms. Shape into evenly sized cake bites (xi) and cool 1–2 hours in the refrigerator, or 20 minutes in the freezer. Dip into white melting chocolate (xii).

MAKES 26-40

Perfect Carrot Cake

Classic flavors are mixed together in this little cake bite. Simply adorable, perfect texture, and amazing flavor. I imagine these cake bites would be great for any gathering, informal or formal—especially for a wedding!

1 box spice cake mix

½ cup finely grated carrots

3 eggs

¼ cup vegetable oil

¾ cup half-and-half

1 tsp. ginger

1 tsp. cinnamon

MIX TOGETHER cake mix, carrots, eggs, vegetable oil, half-and-half, ginger, and cinnamon. Batter will be thick. Pour into a greased 9x13 baking pan. Bake at 350 degrees for 28–32 minutes or until cake springs back when lightly touched. Remove from oven and cool completely. Crumble cake into small, even pieces, placing crumbs in a large bowl.

MAKES 26-40

ADD
8 oz. cream cheese, softened

WITH THE BACK of a spoon, mix together cake crumbles with cream cheese until a thick dough consistency forms. Shape into evenly sized cake bites (xi) and cool 1–2 hours in the refrigerator, or 20 minutes in the freezer. Dip into white melting chocolate (xii). Sprinkle with chopped nuts if desired.

Gingerbread Cookie

1 box spice cake mix

¼ cup molasses

1 cup milk

3 eggs

MIX TOGETHER cake mix, molasses, milk, and eggs. Batter will be thick. Pour into a greased 9x13 baking pan. Bake at 350 degrees for 28–32 minutes or until cake springs back when lightly touched. Remove from oven and cool completely. Crumble cake into small, even pieces, placing crumbs in a large bowl.

ADD

1 cup Cinnamon Vanilla Buttercream Frosting (135)

WITH THE BACK of a spoon, mix together cake crumbles with frosting until a thick dough consistency forms. Shape into evenly sized cake bites (xi) and cool 1–2 hours in the refrigerator, or 20 minutes in the freezer. Dip into white melting chocolate (xii).

MAKES 26-40

Candy Cane

Candy Cane

I think I will leave Santa Claus some of these little cake bites from now on. I've been really good, and will continue to be good. . . . And I'm sure these bites will help.

1 box white cake mix

¾ cup milk

3 eggs

1 tsp. vanilla extract

MIX TOGETHER cake mix, milk, eggs, and vanilla extract. Batter will be thick. Pour into a greased 9x13 baking pan. Bake at 350 degrees for 28–32 minutes or until cake springs back when lightly touched. Remove from oven and cool completely. Crumble cake into small, even pieces, placing crumbs in a large bowl.

ADD

1 cup Vanilla Buttercream Frosting (125)

½ cup crushed candy canes

WITH THE BACK of a spoon, mix together cake crumbles with other ingredients until a thick dough consistency forms. Shape into evenly sized cake bites (xi) and cool 1–2 hours in the refrigerator, or 20 minutes in the freezer. Dip into white melting chocolate (xii). Top with crushed candy canes for garnish if desired.

MAKES 26-40

Pumpkin Cheesecake

This recipe is a "keeper" among all those who taste tested it for me. A perfect combination of pumpkin and cheesecake. Thank you to all my taste testers!

1 box white cake mix

1 cup pumpkin puree

3 eggs

1 tsp. pumpkin pie spice

¾ cup milk

MIX TOGETHER cake mix, pumpkin puree, eggs, spice, and milk. Batter will be thick. Pour into a greased 9x13 baking pan. Bake at 350 degrees for 28–32 minutes or until cake springs back when lightly touched. Remove from oven and cool completely. Crumble cake into small, even pieces, placing crumbs in a large bowl.

ADD

8 oz. cream cheese, softened

⅓ cup pumpkin puree

MAKES 26–40

WITH THE BACK of a spoon, mix together cake crumbles with other ingredients until a thick dough consistency forms. Shape into evenly sized cake bites (xi) and cool 1–2 hours in the refrigerator, or 20 minutes in the freezer. Dip into white melting chocolate (xii).

Caramel Cream

I love caramel candies so much that I usually keep a secret stash in my office . . . but please don't tell my kids. I like having a special snack that's just for me.

1 box butter cake mix

3 eggs

8 Tbsp. (1 stick) butter, melted and cooled

½ cup milk

1 tsp. vanilla extract

MIX TOGETHER cake mix, eggs, butter, milk, and vanilla extract. Batter will be thick. Pour into a greased 9x13 baking pan. Bake at 350 degrees for 28–32 minutes or until cake springs back when lightly touched. Remove from oven and cool completely. Crumble cake into small, even pieces, placing crumbs in a large bowl.

ADD

¾ cup Vanilla Buttercream Frosting (125)

⅓ cup caramel sauce

WITH THE BACK of a spoon, mix together cake crumbles with other ingredients until a thick dough consistency forms. Shape into evenly sized cake bites (xi) and cool 1–2 hours in the refrigerator, or 20 minutes in the freezer. Dip into white melting chocolate (xii). Drizzle with caramel sauce if desired.

MAKES 26-40

Churro

Churro

I am a foodie, through and through. I have favorite foods that remind me of places I go, events I attend, or memories with friends and family that I treasure. For example, the Churro. It reminds me of listening to the sounds of the Napa County Fair, from my grandmother's back porch as a small child, or going to Disneyland . . . one of the happiest places on earth (other than being surrounded by my family at the dinner table).

1 box yellow cake mix

3 eggs

¾ cup milk

¼ cup oil

1 tsp. vanilla extract

MIX TOGETHER cake mix, half-and-half, oil, eggs, and vanilla extract. Batter will be thick. Pour into a greased 9x13 baking pan. Bake at 350 degrees for 28–32 minutes or until cake springs back when lightly touched. Remove from oven and cool completely. Crumble cake into small, even pieces, placing crumbs in a large bowl.

ADD

1 cup Cinnamon Vanilla Buttercream Frosting (135)

WITH THE BACK of a spoon, mix together cake crumbles with frosting until a thick dough consistency forms. Shape into evenly sized cake bites (xi) and cool 1–2 hours in the refrigerator, or 20 minutes in the freezer. Dip into white melting chocolate (xii). Top with a mixture of cinnamon sugar, ½ cup sugar to ½ tsp. cinnamon.

MAKES 26-40

The Nutty Bunch

This cake bite has all the nuts you could ever want. Don't be afraid to substitute the nuts listed for your favorite combination. Creativity is key.

1 box spice cake mix

¼ cup roasted almonds, chopped

¼ cup roasted walnuts, chopped

¼ cup roasted pecans, chopped

3 eggs

1 cup milk

1 tsp. vanilla extract

MIX TOGETHER cake mix, nuts, eggs, milk, and vanilla extract. Batter will be thick. Pour into a greased 9x13 baking pan. Bake at 350 degrees for 28–32 minutes or until cake springs back when lightly touched. Remove from oven and cool completely. Crumble cake into small, even pieces, placing crumbs in a large bowl.

MAKES 26–40

ADD

1 cup Vanilla Buttercream Frosting (125)

WITH THE BACK of a spoon, mix together cake crumbles with frosting until a thick dough consistency forms. Shape into evenly sized cake bites (xi) and cool 1–2 hours in the refrigerator, or 20 minutes in the freezer. Dip into white melting chocolate (xii). Top with more chopped nuts if desired.

Italian Lemon Cream

I love a good dessert! And when I find one, I like to make it in my own kitchen. Thank you to the wonderful Italian Lemon Cream Cake for inspiring me to make my own. Now not only do I save myself money, I can make you and eat you whenever I want.

1 box lemon cream cake mix

3 eggs

2 Tbsp. lemon zest

1 cup milk

MIX TOGETHER cake mix, eggs, lemon zest, and milk. Batter will be thick. Pour into a greased 9x13 baking pan. Bake at 350 degrees for 28–32 minutes or until cake springs back when lightly touched. Remove from oven and cool completely. Crumble cake into small, even pieces, placing crumbs in a large bowl.

ADD

½ cup Lemon Buttercream Frosting (125)

½ cup mascarpone cheese, soft

⅓ cup crushed hard lemon candies

WITH THE BACK of a spoon, mix together cake crumbles with other ingredients until a thick dough consistency forms. Shape into evenly sized cake bites (xi) and cool 1–2 hours in the refrigerator, or 20 minutes in the freezer. Dip into white melting chocolate (xii). Top with crushed lemon candies if desired.

MAKES 26–40

It's a Secret

It's a Secret

The bad thing about making great desserts is sometimes you don't want to say what is inside until after everyone has eaten and loved every last bite. This cake is one of those recipes. . . . "Yeah, honey, I'm glad you loved these cake bites. . . . What's in them, you ask? Well, I'm not really at liberty to tell you. I'll have to kill you if I do."

1 box spice cake mix

½ cup prunes, chopped

3 eggs

1 cup milk

1 tsp. cinnamon

1 tsp. vanilla extract

HINT: Soak prunes in hot water for 20 minutes to soften. Remove from water and coarsely chop.

MIX TOGETHER cake mix, prunes, eggs, milk, cinnamon, and vanilla extract. Batter will be thick. Pour into a greased 9x13 baking pan. Bake at 350 degrees for 28–32 minutes or until cake springs back when lightly touched. Remove from oven and cool completely. Crumble cake into small, even pieces, placing crumbs in a large bowl.

MAKES 26-40

ADD
1 cup Vanilla Buttercream Frosting (125)

WITH THE BACK of a spoon, mix together cake crumbles with frosting until a thick dough consistency forms. Shape into evenly sized cake bites (xi) and cool 1–2 hours in the refrigerator, or 20 minutes in the freezer. Dip into white melting chocolate (xii).

New York Cheesecake

1 box white cake mix

3 eggs

1 cup half-and-half

1 tsp. vanilla extract

MIX TOGETHER cake mix, eggs, half-and-half, and vanilla extract. Batter will be thick. Pour into a greased 9x13 baking pan. Bake at 350 degrees for 28–32 minutes or until cake springs back when lightly touched. Remove from oven and cool completely. Crumble cake into small, even pieces, placing crumbs in a large bowl.

ADD

8 oz. cream cheese, softened

¼ cup Vanilla Buttercream Frosting (125)

WITH THE BACK of a spoon, mix together cake crumbles with other ingredients until a thick dough consistency forms. Shape into evenly sized cake bites (xi) and cool 1–2 hours in the refrigerator, or 20 minutes in the freezer. Dip into white melting chocolate (xii).

MAKES 26-40

German Almond

This is such a great cake bite, I don't know what to say. This may even have me speechless . . . which doesn't happen that often. Ask my husband.

1 box butter cake mix

3 eggs

1 cup half-and-half

2 tsp. almond extract

⅓ cup melted butter

4 Tbsp. almond flour

MIX TOGETHER cake mix, eggs, half-and-half, almond extract, melted butter, and almond flour. Batter will be thick. Pour into a greased 9x13 baking pan. Bake at 350 degrees for 28–32 minutes or until cake springs back when lightly touched. Remove from oven and cool completely. Crumble cake into small, even pieces, placing crumbs in a large bowl.

ADD

1 cup Vanilla Buttercream Frosting (125)

1 tsp. almond extract

MAKES 26–40

WITH THE BACK of a spoon, mix together cake crumbles with other ingredients until a thick dough consistency forms. Shape into evenly sized cake bites (xi) and cool 1–2 hours in the refrigerator, or 20 minutes in the freezer. Dip into white melting chocolate (xii).

French Toast

French Toast

I firmly believe that it's important to have treats for breakfast every now and then. Usually more "now" than "then."

1 box white cake mix

3 eggs

1 cup half-and-half

1 tsp. nutmeg

MIX TOGETHER cake mix, eggs, half-and-half, and nutmeg. Batter will be thick. Pour into a greased 9x13 baking pan. Bake at 350 degrees for 28–32 minutes or until cake springs back when lightly touched. Remove from oven and cool completely. Crumble cake into small, even pieces, placing crumbs in a large bowl.

ADD

1 cup Maple Buttercream Frosting (132)

WITH THE BACK of a spoon, mix together cake crumbles with other ingredients until a thick dough consistency forms. Shape into evenly sized cake bites (xi) and cool 1–2 hours in the refrigerator, or 20 minutes in the freezer. Dip into white melting chocolate (xii). Sprinkle with maple sugar if desired and top with cooked, chopped bacon. Perfection.

MAKES 26-40

Rosemary Lavender

Savory and sweet is an unexpected surprise . . . especially wrapped inside a sweet chocolate candy coating. Shaped like a little ball, this cake bite is perfect for a Sunday brunch or gathering of girlfriends.

1 box white cake mix

3 eggs

½ cup vegetable oil

½ cup milk

1 tsp. vanilla extract

2 Tbsp. dried crushed rosemary

2 Tbsp. dried crushed lavender

MIX TOGETHER cake mix, eggs, oil, milk, vanilla extract, rosemary, and lavender. Batter will be thick. Pour into a greased 9×13 baking pan. Bake at 350 degrees for 28–32 minutes or until cake springs back when lightly touched. Remove from oven and cool completely. Crumble cake into small, even pieces, placing crumbs in a large bowl.

ADD

1 cup Vanilla Buttercream Frosting (125)

MAKES 26–40

WITH THE BACK of a spoon, mix together cake crumbles with frosting until a thick dough consistency forms. Shape into evenly sized cake bites (xi) and cool 1–2 hours in the refrigerator, or 20 minutes in the freezer. Dip into white melting chocolate (xii).

Spicy Red Hot

This time I am not referring to my husband—even though he is pretty darn handsome, especially in those jeans. This time I'm thinking of one of my favorite candies of all time . . . Red Hots.

1 box white cake mix

3 eggs

1 cup milk

1 tsp. vanilla extract

1 tsp. cinnamon

MIX TOGETHER cake mix, eggs, milk, vanilla extract, and cinnamon. Batter will be thick. Pour into a greased 9x13 baking pan. Bake at 350 degrees for 28–32 minutes or until cake springs back when lightly touched. Remove from oven and cool completely. Crumble cake into small, even pieces, placing crumbs in a large bowl.

ADD

1 cup Vanilla Buttercream Frosting (125)

½ cup finely chopped Red Hot candies

WITH THE BACK of a spoon, mix together cake crumbles with other ingredients until a thick dough consistency forms. Shape into evenly sized cake bites (xi) and cool 1–2 hours in the refrigerator, or 20 minutes in the freezer. Dip into white melting chocolate (xii).

MAKES 26-40

St. Patty's Day

St. Patty's Day

Give these cake bites as good luck for St. Patty's Day. They are tasty little treats that are also beautiful.

HINT: when rolling these cake bites, be sure to wear gloves, or your hands will be as green as the grass!

1 box white cake mix

3 eggs

1 cup half-and-half

1 tsp. vanilla extract

1 oz. liquid green food coloring

½ cup sour cream

MIX TOGETHER cake mix, eggs, half-and-half, vanilla extract, and sour cream. Batter will be thick. Pour into a greased 9x13 baking pan. Bake at 350 degrees for 28–32 minutes or until cake springs back when lightly touched. Remove from oven and cool completely. Crumble cake into small, even pieces, placing crumbs in a large bowl.

ADD

8 oz. cream cheese, softened

¼–½ cup Vanilla Buttercream Frosting (125)

MAKES 26-40

WITH THE BACK of a spoon, mix together cake crumbles with other ingredients until a thick dough consistency forms. Shape into evenly sized cake bites (xi) and cool 1–2 hours in the refrigerator, or 20 minutes in the freezer. Dip into white melting chocolate (xii). Sprinkle with green nonpareils or green edible glitter.

Orange Cranberry

When it's harvest time, the leaves are changing, the air is cooler, and these flavors tend to be in my kitchen every day. It's a perfect pairing of fall flavors, rich with beautiful colors.

1 box yellow cake mix

3 Tbsp. orange juice

1 tsp. orange extract

2 Tbsp. grated orange zest

3 eggs

¾ cup milk

Orange food coloring (2–3 drops)

MIX TOGETHER cake mix, orange juice, orange extract, orange zest, eggs, and milk. Add food coloring to desired orange color. Batter will be thick. Pour into a greased 9x13 baking pan. Bake at 350 degrees for 28–32 minutes or until cake springs back when lightly touched. Remove from oven and cool completely. Crumble cake into small, even pieces, placing crumbs in a large bowl.

MAKES 26-40

ADD

1 cup Cream Cheese Frosting (131)

½ cup finely chopped dried cranberries

WITH THE BACK of a spoon, mix together cake crumbles with other ingredients until a thick dough consistency forms. Shape into evenly sized cake bites (xi) and cool 1–2 hours in the refrigerator, or 20 minutes in the freezer. Dip into white or orange melting chocolate (xii).

Theme Decorating

Roll the Dice!

Roll the Dice!

For game night, these little cake bites will be the perfect treat! You can even do cake pops for added flair! Let's roll!

1 recipe cake bites or cake pops, prepared and ready to dip (xi)

1 lb. white melting chocolate

2 Tbsp. vegetable oil

Black food coloring pen

HEAT WHITE melting chocolate per directions on package. Add 2 tablespoons vegetable oil and stir to combine with warm chocolate.

USING YOUR hands, form one cake bite into a cube. Dip into white chocolate, covering all sides. Gently tap cake bite until excess chocolate slides off. Set cake bite on wax paper until chocolate firms. Repeat for entire batch.

USING YOUR black food coloring pen, mark dots on each side, leaving one side unmarked. Place that side down on the platter, or have this be the side where the candy stick has been placed.

MAKES 26-40

Scrabble

Scrabble

My sister-in-law loves scrabble. In fact, I think she studies before the family scrabble game nights. I've beaten her only two times in the seven years I've known her. Maybe I can sweeten my chances by making these for her? Do you think she'll go easy on me now? Probably not, but it's worth a try.

1 recipe cake bites or cake pops, prepared and ready to dip (xi)

1 lb. white melting chocolate

2 Tbsp. vegetable oil

1 package soft caramels, rolled thin and cut into squares.

Black food coloring pen, or gel pen

MIX TOGETHER melting chocolate per directions on package. Add 2 tablespoons vegetable oil and stir to combine with warm chocolate. Using your hand, flatten a cake bite and form into the shape of an alphabet tile. Dip into white chocolate, covering all sides. Gently tap cake bite until excess chocolate slides off. Set cake bite on wax paper until chocolate firms. Repeat for entire batch.

USING YOUR melting chocolate as your glue, place thin caramel squares on the cake bites. Once secure, write a letter on each cake bite with your black food coloring pen or gel pen, along with the corresponding number point for each letter. For added creativity, use the lettering to create a message or clue for your guests.

MAKES 26–40

Life's a Beach

Life's a Beach

Certainly worthy of any luau or beach party, these themed cake bites are cute as can be.

1 recipe cake bites or cake pops, prepared and ready to dip (xi)

Cake bite recipe suggestions: Piña Colada (5) or Key Lime Pie (3)

1 lb. white melting chocolate

2 Tbsp. vegetable oil

Raw sugar

Small drink umbrellas

MIX TOGETHER melting chocolate per directions on package. Add 2 tablespoons vegetable oil and stir to combine with warm chocolate. Dip into white chocolate, covering all sides. Gently tap cake bite until excess chocolate slides off. Next, dip cake bite into raw sugar, covering cake bite to look like a sandy beach. Top with a small drink umbrella. Set cake bite on wax paper until chocolate firms.

MAKES 26-40

Scary Ghost

Scary Ghost

For those of us who can be decorating-challenged at times, why not use a small cookie cutter before cooling your cake bites to help shape them into something special? It's fast, foolproof, and will knock the socks off your guests.

1 recipe cake bites or cake pops, prepared, shaped into ghosts, and ready to dip (xi)

1 lb. white melting chocolate

2 Tbsp. vegetable oil

Black food coloring pen or black gel pen

HEAT WHITE melting chocolate per directions on package. Add 2 tablespoons vegetable oil and stir to combine with warm chocolate. Dip into white chocolate, covering all sides. Gently tap cake bite until excess chocolate slides off. Set cake bite on wax paper until chocolate firms. Then, using your black food coloring pen or gel pen, make the eyes and mouth of your ghost.

MAKES 26–40

Plump Turkey

Plump Turkey

These cake bites or pops are a great place setting idea for your next Thanksgiving feast. They will serve 2 purposes—crafty cuteness and a tasty after- or before-dinner treat!

1 recipe cake bites or cake pops, prepared, shaped into turkeys, and ready to dip (xi)

Cake bite recipe suggestions: Sweet Potato Pie (67), Pumpkin Pie (80), or Harvest Pumpkin (69)

1 lb. dark melting chocolate

2 Tbsp. vegetable oil

Small pretzels

Whole almonds or candy corn

Small white round nonpareils

Black food coloring pen or black gel pen

HEAT DARK melting chocolate per directions on package. Add 2 tablespoons vegetable oil and stir to combine with warm chocolate. Dip cake bite into white chocolate, covering all sides. Gently tap cake bite until excess chocolate slides off. Set on wax paper until chocolate firms.

OR IF you are going to make a cake pop, slide the pretzel up the stick and press firmly to the wet chocolate until it sets. These are the feet. Using the melting chocolate as your glue, place the almonds or candy corn for the beak and feathers and the white nonpareils for the eyes. Let set. Then use your black food coloring pen to finish the eyes.

MAKES 26–40

True Love

When you theme your treats, it makes them all the more special. You've taken the time to make a treat with love, and that is one of the best presents you can give to another—something that's made with love.

1 recipe cake bites or cake pops, prepared and ready to dip (xi)

Cake bite recipe suggestions: Southern Red Velvet (75), Cherry Cordial (37), or Dark Chocolate Truffle (35)

1 lb. red or pastel melting chocolate

2 Tbsp. vegetable oil

Edible red glitter

Red ribbon

Black food coloring pen or black gel pen

OR

½ lb. each pink, lavender, light green, or yellow melting chocolate

1–4 Tbsp. vegetable oil

White food coloring pen or white gel pen

Pastel ribbon

MAKES 26–40

HINT: I highly recommend doing this cake bite as a cake pop. Follow the instructions on (x).

HEAT MELTING chocolate per directions on package. Add 1 tablespoon vegetable oil to each color of melting chocolate (in separate bowls) and stir to combine with warm chocolate. With a small heart shaped cookie cutter (approx 1½ in.), shape the cake bite and make a cake pop (x).

DIP INTO chocolate, covering all sides. Gently tap cake bite until excess chocolate slides off. Decorate with sprinkles if desired. Set cake bite on wax paper until chocolate firms. Then using your food coloring pen or gel pen, write love messages on the center front of the hearts. Use ribbon to embellish the sticks.

Easter Egg

Another great spring treat, I received the inspiration for this cake bite from some Easter candy I purchased last year. They are beautiful and tasty—the pastel colors bring spring to a reality. . . . Even if there is still snow on the ground.

1 recipe cake bites or cake pops, prepared and ready to dip (xi)

½ lb. each white, pink, and yellow melting chocolate

3 Tbsp. vegetable oil

Sprinkles to coordinate with your melting chocolate

HEAT MELTING chocolate per directions on package. Add 1 tablespoon vegetable oil to each color of melting chocolate (in separate bowls) and stir to combine with warm chocolate. With your hands, shape the cake bite into an oval, or like an egg. Dip into white chocolate, covering all sides. Gently tap cake bite until excess chocolate slides off. Decorate with sprinkles much like you would your Easter eggs. Set cake bite on wax paper until chocolate firms.

MAKES 26-40

Spring Flowers

Spring Flowers

After a long, cold winter, I am always anxious for spring to arrive. Just like seeing your first bloom in the garden, these cake bites will bring a smile to your face. Happy spring!

1 recipe cake bites or cake pops, prepared and ready to dip (xi)

Cake bite recipe suggestions: Pink Lemonade (12), Strawberry Shortcake (16), Lemon Cream Pie (8), or St. Patty's Day (95)

1 lb. green melting chocolate or candy coating

2 Tbsp. vegetable oil

Pastel gumdrops, small round

Pastel candy corns, variety of colors

HEAT GREEN melting chocolate per directions on package. Add 2 tablespoons vegetable oil and stir to combine with warm chocolate. Using round cake balls, shaped and ready to dip, or cake pops (whatever your heart desires), dip into green chocolate, covering all sides. Gently tap cake bite until excess chocolate slides off. Set on wax paper until chocolate firms.

Once your cake bite or pop is dry, use your warm melting chocolate as your glue to place a small gumdrop in the center or side of the round cake bite or pop, sliced in half. Next take your pastel candy corn, one at a time, dipping bottom pointed side into the warm melting chocolate, and press gently next to the round gumdrop center. Hold firm for 20 seconds or until the chocolate sets. Repeat with all the candy corn, until the petals of the flower take shape. You can place them on a foam round covered in moss, or in a vase for display. Perfect for Mother's Day or a get-well gift.

MAKES 26-40

Football

Football

These cake bites are for my son. He has become our sports enthusiast, and I am happiest when I sit and watch NFL football with him. His dream is to become the New England Patriots quarterback. I'll be the one cheering the loudest from the sidelines—and feeding the team cake bites after the game. . . . Can you imagine how many cake bites I'll have to make?

1 recipe cake bites or cake pops, prepared and ready to dip (xi)

1 lb. dark melting chocolate

2 Tbsp. vegetable oil

White gel pen

HEAT DARK melting chocolate per directions on package. Add 2 tablespoons vegetable oil and stir to combine with warm chocolate. Shape cake bite into an oval with pointed ends (like a football). Dip into dark chocolate, covering all sides. Gently tap cake bite until excess chocolate slides off.

SET CAKE BITE in a foam block until chocolate firms. Use your white gel pen to draw the white laces of the football or any other desired marking.

MAKES 26–40

Love at First Bite

Love at First Bite

This cake bite needs the Southern Red Velvet recipe (75) to do it justice. Trust me, the dark red smooth cake is irresistible—especially for you vampire fans. Simply stunning.

1 recipe cake bites or cake pops, prepared and ready to dip (xi)

Cake bite recipe suggestions: Southern Red Velvet (75)

1 lb. white melting chocolate

2 Tbsp. vegetable oil

White or clear edible glitter

HEAT WHITE melting chocolate per directions on package. Add 2 tablespoons vegetable oil to warm chocolate and stir to combine. Dip into white chocolate, covering all sides. Gently tap cake bite until excess chocolate slides off. Immediately sprinkle with edible glitter. Set cake bite on wax paper until chocolate firms.

MAKES 26-40

Spooky Eyes

Spooky Eyes

I did these cake bites for Halloween, and they were so creepy I almost didn't want to eat them. I said almost. They are phenomenal. Really.

1 recipe cake bites or cake pops, prepared and ready to dip (xi)

Cake bite recipe suggestions: Southern Red Velvet (75)

1 lb. white melting chocolate

2 Tbsp. vegetable oil

Brown chocolate candies

Red food coloring pen or red gel pen

HEAT WHITE melting chocolate per directions on package. Add 2 tablespoons vegetable oil to melting chocolate and stir to combine. Dip into white chocolate, covering all sides. Gently tap cake bite until excess chocolate slides off. Place chocolate candy in the center top of cake bite. Set cake bite on wax paper until chocolate firms. Then use your red food coloring pen or gel pen to draw blood vessels on each eye ball.

MAKES 26-40

Pea in the Pod

Pea in the Pod

Alison, you are my creative inspiration. I love your ideas, and I'm glad that we came up with this little pea-in-a-pod idea. It's cute, loveable, and perfect. Thank you!

1 recipe cake bites or cake pops, prepared and ready to dip (xi)

Cake bite recipe suggestions: St. Patty's Day (95) or Key Lime Pie (3)

1 lb. dark or light green melting chocolate

2 Tbsp. vegetable oil

Black food coloring pen or black gel pen

Green card stock or green half moon shaped gumdrops

White foam block

Artificial grass

HINT: I highly recommend doing this cake bite as a cake pop. Follow the instructions on page x.

HEAT GREEN melting chocolate per directions on package. Add 2 tablespoons vegetable oil to melting chocolate and stir to combine. Dip cake bite into green chocolate, covering all sides. Gently tap cake bite until excess chocolate slides off. Set cake bite on wax paper until chocolate firms. Color eyes with black food coloring pen. Cut out the shape of a pea pod using your green card stock or slide a green half moon shape gumdrop up the stick of the cake pop, centering it. If using card stock, gently tape it onto each cake pop stick. Place in foam or artificial grass for presentation.

MAKES 26-40

My Little Princess

My Little Princess

Every princess deserves a magic wand! These star wands are not only perfect for a princess themed party, but also an award show or a "you are special" treat. They can make any girl feel like a princess . . . regardless of her age!

1 recipe cake bites or cake pops, prepared and ready to dip (xi)

Cake bite recipe suggestions: Pink Lemonade (12)

HINT: I highly recommend doing this cake bite as a cake pop (x).

1 lb. dark or light pink melting chocolate

2 Tbsp. vegetable oil

Edible pink glitter

pink ribbon

HEAT PINK melting chocolate per directions on package. Add 2 tablespoons vegetable oil to melting chocolate and stir to combine. Dip into pink chocolate, covering all sides. Gently tap cake bite until excess chocolate slides off. Sprinkle with edible glitter. Set on wax paper until chocolate firms. Tie some pretty pink ribbon around the base of the cake pop. . . . Leave strands to curl or tie in a bow.

MAKES 26-40

O, Christmas Tree

Tis the season for cute festive treats. These little Christmas trees are picture perfect, super simple, and you can customize them to your liking!

1 recipe cake bites or cake pops, prepared and ready to dip (xi)

Cake bite recipe suggestions: St. Patty's Day (95), Egg Nog (63), or Candy Cane (79)

1 lb. dark or light green melting chocolate

2 Tbsp. vegetable oil

Sprinkles (in as many sizes and colors as your heart desires)

HINT: I highly recommend doing this cake bite as a cake pop (x).

HEAT GREEN melting chocolate per directions on package. Add 2 tablespoons vegetable oil to melting chocolate and stir to combine. Shape cake bite into a triangle shape, such as a Christmas tree. Dip into green chocolate, covering all sides. Gently tap cake bite until excess chocolate slides off. Place sprinkles in diagonal rows. Set cake bite on wax paper until chocolate firms.

MAKES 26–40

The Icing Inside the Little Bites

Chocolate Ganache

1 cup heavy whipping cream

12 ounces semi-sweet chocolate chunks or chips

HEAT THE cream in a saucepan until it comes to a boil.

REMOVE CREAM and pour over chocolate in a mixing bowl.

STIR TO mix together.

POUR OVER warm cakes or allow to cool slightly and spread like frosting.

MAKES 3 Cups

Vanilla Buttercream

8 Tbsp. (1 stick) butter, room temperature

3¾ cups powdered sugar, sifted

3–4 Tbsp. milk or cream

2 tsp. vanilla extract

PLACE BUTTER in a large mixing bowl. Beat until light and fluffy, about 30 seconds. Stop the mixer before adding the sugar or you will have a large mess to clean up.

ADD SUGAR, 3 tablespoons milk (or cream), and vanilla extract. Beat frosting, starting on slow and increasing your speed until frosting is nice and creamy. Add 1 or more tablespoons of milk (or cream) if frosting is too thick.

MAKES 3 Cups

Chocolate Buttercream

8 Tbsp. (1 stick) butter, room temperature

3¾ cups powdered sugar, sifted

⅓ cup cocoa

3–4 Tbsp. milk or cream

2 tsp. vanilla extract

PLACE BUTTER in a large mixing bowl. Beat until light and fluffy, about 30 seconds. Stop the mixer before adding the sugar and cocoa or you will have a large mess to clean up.

ADD SUGAR, cocoa, 3 tablespoons milk (or cream), and vanilla extract. Beat frosting, starting on slow and increasing your speed until frosting is nice and creamy. Add 1 or more tablespoons of milk (or cream) if frosting is too thick.

MAKES 3 Cups

Root Beer Buttercream

8 Tbsp. (1 stick) butter, room temperature

3¾ cups powdered sugar, sifted

3–4 Tbsp. milk or cream

1 tsp. root beer flavoring

PLACE BUTTER in a large mixing bowl. Beat until light and fluffy, about 30 seconds. Stop the mixer before adding the sugar or you will have a large mess to clean up.

ADD SUGAR, 3 tablespoons milk (or cream), and root beer flavoring. Beat frosting, starting on slow and increasing your speed until frosting is nice and creamy. Add 1 or more tablespoons of milk (or cream) if frosting is too thick.

MAKES 3 Cups

Caramel Cream

4 Tbsp. (½ stick) butter

¼ cup brown sugar

¼ cup dark brown sugar

2–3 Tbsp. whole milk

1 cup powdered sugar

1 tsp. vanilla extract

PLACE BUTTER and brown sugars in a medium skillet over medium heat. Stir and cook the mixture until it comes to a boil.

ADD MILK and bring the mixture back to a boil, stirring constantly. Remove the pan from the heat and add the powdered sugar and vanilla. Beat mixture with a wooden spoon until smooth and creamy. Frosting will harden when cooled completely.

MAKES 3 Cups

Mint Chocolate Buttercream

8 Tbsp. (1 stick) butter, room temperature

3¾ cups powdered sugar, sifted

3–4 Tbsp. milk or cream

1 tsp. mint extract

1 cup finely chopped semi-sweet chocolate

PLACE BUTTER in a large mixing bowl. Beat until light and fluffy, about 30 seconds. Stop the mixer before adding the sugar or you will have a large mess to clean up.

ADD SUGAR, 3 tablespoons milk (or cream), and mint extract. Beat frosting, starting on slow and increasing your speed until frosting is nice and creamy. Add 1 or more tablespoons of milk (or cream) if frosting is too thick. Add 1 cup finely chopped chocolate into frosting.

MAKES 3 Cups

Lime Buttercream

8 Tbsp. (1 stick) butter, room temperature

3¾ cups powdered sugar, sifted

3–4 Tbsp. milk or cream

2 tsp. lime extract or lime juice

2 Tbsp. lime zest

PLACE BUTTER in a large mixing bowl. Beat until light and fluffy, about 30 seconds. Stop the mixer before adding the sugar or you will have a large mess to clean up.

ADD SUGAR, 3 tablespoons milk (or cream), lime extract or juice, and lime zest. Beat frosting, starting on slow and increasing your speed until frosting is nice and creamy. Add 1 or more tablespoons of milk (or cream) if frosting is too thick.

MAKES 3 Cups

Cream Cheese

8 oz. cream cheese, softened

8 Tbsp. (1 stick) butter, softened

3¾ cups powdered sugar

1 tsp. vanilla

BEAT CREAM CHEESE and butter until smooth and light. Stop the mixer and add sugar and vanilla extract. Beat frosting, starting on slow and increasing your speed until frosting is nice and creamy.

ADD 1 or more tablespoons of milk (or cream) if frosting is too thick. Keep this frosting (and any treats you frost with it) refrigerated.

MAKES 3 Cups

Maple Buttercream

1½ tsp. maple flavoring

8 Tbsp. (1 stick) butter

3 Tbsp. cream

3¾ cups. powdered sugar

IN A large mixer, add maple flavoring, butter, and cream, beating on medium until smooth. Stop mixer and add half of the powdered sugar. Beat frosting, starting on low speed until powdered sugar is incorporated. Stop mixer and add remaining powdered sugar until the frosting reaches desired texture. You may also add more cream if needed, 1 tablespoon at a time.

MAKES 3 Cups

Coconut Buttercream

8 Tbsp. (1 stick) butter, room temperature

3¾ cups powdered sugar, sifted

3–4 Tbsp. coconut milk or cream

2 tsp. coconut extract

PLACE BUTTER in a large mixing bowl. Beat until light and fluffy, about 30 seconds. Stop the mixer before adding the sugar or you will have a large mess to clean up.

ADD SUGAR, 3 tablespoons coconut milk (or cream), and coconut extract. Beat frosting, starting on slow and increasing your speed until frosting is nice and creamy. Add 1 or more tablespoons of milk (or cream) if frosting is too thick.

MAKES 3 Cups

Browned Butter

1 stick butter

4 cups powdered sugar

1 tsp. vanilla

½ cup heavy cream or more desired consistency

IN A small skillet, brown butter over medium heat until golden brown flecks appear. Butter will become a little foamy. Stir now and then to make sure the butter cooks evenly. Remove from heat and cool slightly.

ADD POWDERED sugar, vanilla, and cream. Beat on medium high until a creamy texture to your liking forms.

MAKES 3 Cups

Cinnamon Vanilla Buttercream

8 Tbsp. (1 stick) butter, room temperature

3¾ cups powdered sugar, sifted

3–4 Tbsp. milk or cream

2 tsp. vanilla extract

1 Tbsp. cinnamon

PLACE BUTTER in a large mixing bowl. Beat until light and fluffy, about 30 seconds. Stop the mixer before adding the sugar or you will have a large mess to clean up.

ADD SUGAR, 3 tablespoons milk (or cream), and vanilla extract. Beat frosting, starting on slow and increasing your speed until frosting is nice and creamy. Stir in cinnamon. Add 1 or more tablespoons of milk (or cream) if frosting is too thick.

MAKES 3 Cups

Peanut Butter

8 Tbsp. (1 stick) butter, room temperature

1 cup peanut butter (chunky or smooth—I prefer smooth)

2 cups powdered sugar

3–4 Tbsp. milk or cream

1 tsp. vanilla extract

COMBINE BUTTER and peanut butter in a large bowl, mixing together until light and fluffy. Stop the mixer before adding the sugar.

ADD SUGAR, 3 tablespoons of milk (or cream), and vanilla. Beat frosting, starting on slow and increasing your speed until frosting is nice and creamy. Add 1 or more tablespoons of milk (or cream) if frosting is too thick.

MAKES 3 Cups

Lemon Buttercream

8 Tbsp. (1 stick) butter, room temperature

3¾ cups powdered sugar, sifted

3–4 Tbsp. milk or cream

2 tsp. lemon extract

PLACE BUTTER in a large mixing bowl. Beat until light and fluffy, about 30 seconds. Stop the mixer before adding the sugar or you will have a large mess to clean up.

ADD SUGAR, 3 tablespoons milk (or cream), and lemon extract. Beat frosting, starting on slow and increasing your speed until frosting is nice and creamy. Add 1 or more tablespoons of milk (or cream) if frosting is too thick.

MAKES 3 Cups

Rum Buttercream

8 Tbsp. (1 stick) butter, room temperature

3¾ cups powdered sugar, sifted

3–4 Tbsp. milk or cream

2 tsp. rum extract

PLACE BUTTER in a large mixing bowl. Beat until light and fluffy, about 30 seconds. Stop the mixer before adding the sugar or you will have a large mess to clean up.

ADD SUGAR, 3 tablespoons milk (or cream), and rum extract. Beat frosting, starting on slow and increasing your speed until frosting is nice and creamy. Add 1 or more tablespoons of milk (or cream) if frosting is too thick.

MAKES 3 Cups

Cookies and Cream Buttercream

8 Tbsp. (1 stick) butter, room temperature

3¾ cups powdered sugar, sifted

3–4 Tbsp. milk or cream

2 tsp. vanilla extract

⅓ cup crushed chocolate sandwich cookies

PLACE BUTTER in a large mixing bowl. Beat until light and fluffy, about 30 seconds. Stop the mixer before adding the sugar or you will have a large mess to clean up.

ADD SUGAR, 3 tablespoons milk (or cream), and vanilla extract. Beat frosting, starting on slow and increasing your speed until frosting is nice and creamy. Add the crushed cookies. If the frosting is too thick, you can add 1 or more tablespoons of milk (or cream).

MAKES 3 Cups

Custard Cream

8 Tbsp. (1 stick) butter, room temperature

3¾ cups powdered sugar, sifted

3–4 Tbsp. milk or cream

2 tsp. vanilla extract

2 Tbsp. Bird's Custard Powder

PLACE BUTTER in a large mixing bowl. Beat until light and fluffy, about 30 seconds. Stop the mixer before adding the sugar or you will have a large mess to clean up.

ADD SUGAR, 3 tablespoons milk (or cream), and vanilla extract. Beat frosting, starting on slow and increasing your speed until frosting is nice and creamy. Add Bird's Custard Powder. If the frosting is too thick, you can add 1 or more tablespoons of milk (or cream).

MAKES 3 Cups

Raspberry Buttercream

8 Tbsp. (1 stick) butter, room temperature

3¾ cups powdered sugar, sifted

3–4 Tbsp. milk or cream

2 tsp. raspberry extract

PLACE BUTTER in a large mixing bowl. Beat until light and fluffy, about 30 seconds. Stop the mixer before adding the sugar or you will have a large mess to clean up.

ADD SUGAR, 3 tablespoons milk (or cream), and raspberry extract. Beat frosting, starting on slow and increasing your speed until frosting is nice and creamy. Add 1 or more tablespoons of milk (or cream) if frosting is too thick.

MAKES 3 Cups

Recipe Index

recipe index

About the Author

WENDY L. PAUL has been cooking and baking for many years. She enjoys writing new recipes and creating easy-to-make dinners and desserts. Her baking skills have been featured on numerous morning TV shows and news programs. When Wendy is working on a project—whether home improvement, a new recipe, or shopping at a craft store—she is truly happy. She is the bestselling author of *101 Gourmet Cupcakes in 10 Minutes* and *101 Gourmet Cookies for Everyone*. She and her family live in Utah, and oddly enough have a dog named Cupcake. For more information, visit her website at www.wendypaulcreations.com.

About the Photographer

MARIELLE HAYES is a photographer based in the San Francisco Bay Area. When she is not behind the camera, she enjoys traveling and spending time with her friends and family. She resides in the Oakland Hills with her husband, daughter, and Boston Terrier dog.